49+1

Poems

Dan Dunklee

The Barn
Clovis, CA.

49+1 Copyright © 2022 Daniel Dunklee

All rights reserved. No part of this book may be used or reproduced in any manner whatsoever without written permission from the publisher, except in the case of brief quotations embodied in critical articles or reviews.

Library of Congress Control Number: 2022916325

ISBN:
978-1-952467-16-5 Paperback

Oct 2022

Production assistance from The Barn

The Barn
Clovis, CA.

Poem Number —Contents — First Line

1......quality and quantity	1
2 ...... voices in the water	5
3 ...... shadows beacon the comfort	6
4 ...... words without meaning	8
5 ...... where is the sunset	10
6 ...... summer begins with a quiet rush	11
7 ...... golden dreams washed with	12
8 ...... steeped canyon walls	14
9 ...... clouds carry the message	17
10 ...... chasing butterflies	18
11 ...... walking with the illustrators	20
12 ...... an iris in full bloom	22
13 ...... tell me your name	24
14 ...... county dances held in the neighbors barn	27
15 ...... miracles persist in alienating the soul	28
16 ...... seaside vistas explored on a whim	30
17 ...... sequined gowns form the basics of illusion	32
18 ...... owl woman goes walking	33
19 ...... silent strings	38
20 ...... she sits at the turnstile	40
21 ...... close your eyes	43
22 ...... the first time we ever saw the sunset	47
23 ...... she stands there just watching	48
24 ...... stepping stones blanket the garden path	51
25 ...... did you ever think	52

26	the dancers whirl to	54
27	sage bends as	55
28	she stands at the edge	58
29	glowing embers	61
30	powder soft	64
31	questions go unanswered	66
32	i stand naked in the moonlight	67
33	a slight bend in the river	69
34	visions	70
35	prisms glistening	72
36	Do you remember?	74
37	When we're sixty- four, a very interesting thought.	76
38	dreams	78
39	Brute force	81
40	dark stormy clouds threaten	82
41	laying here	84
42	sarcastic remarks	86
43	canoe	89
44	sequined dreams dance in the moonlight	91
45	secret gardens full	93
46	iron pickets	96
47	flickering light from a candlestick	97
48	soft lace	98
49	growth cumulated with understanding	100
+1	I'm an old man.	102

1

EDIBLE ARMOR

quality and quantity
    measured as a microcosm
    with no thought given to action or reaction
    only to mask what has lain dormant
    what has been buried by the teachings
    the ravings of the lunatics
    in caps and gowns
    collars and robes

    chainmail wrought in the furnaces of emotions
    and the supposed expectations of the world
    barriers built for protection
    end up hiding the one from the self
    sometimes too deep to retrieve

    such are the devices used to mask emotions

    built link by link
    to ensure solitude
    and to restrict judgements

a boisterous laugh
a look of disgust
telling of what is wrong
and condemning all that is unfamiliar

placements being made
one brick at a time
to encompass dreams and wishes
judged unsuitable by the masses
or the individuals own skepticisms

teaching the very young the mistrust
we all cherish
corruptions we feel necessary to exist
in this passage of time we call living

dissolving the wide eyed wonder of nature
by can't's and shouldn'ts
destroying acceptance
with judgements passed from
parent, teacher and cleric
generations to infinity

such are the devices used to mask emotions
built link by link
to ensure solitude
and restrict judgements
armor encasing
invisible and impenetrable
by the outside until seen by the pure
with no need for judgements

the change begins within
slowly gnawing and consuming
opening and spreading the cleavage
to acceptance

as rust eats metal
the armor is edible

2

voices in the water
    mixing acapella
    keeping their own rhythm
    adding percussion with the stones

wind whispers
playing havoc in the trees
come here little one
protection is within the mother

the earth so pleasant
engulfing
taking back what was on loan

the body used as nutrients
for the smaller
the soul released to move on

3

shadows beacon the comfort
   a place to hide from
   the wondering glances
   raised eyebrows of contempt and jealousy

   judgements formulated
   without questioning
   authenticity

   condemning

   the touch of a man to a man
   a woman to a woman
   the need sometimes so great
   it seems overpowering

   sex and gender
   seldom mix

   the occurrence of both within the same body
   causes acceptance and understanding
   passion and unequaled love
   commitment is given to those deserving
   those part of the whole

how many souls to make one
one, two, three, a million

how can love be reserved
kept in a cedar chest
under lock and key

handle with care
the emotions of the mixed
some are strong in the face of danger
only to crumble when touched by love

how can one choose
when both paths run parallel
the treats delicious on both sides
why can't one straddle and be both

what is man
what is woman

aren't they both the same?

4

words without meaning
    poured forth effortlessly
    filling the paper with
    nothing more than words

    no question
    no answers
    no hidden meaning
    just words

    coming from deep within
    are these revealing cliche's
    dark secrets and hopes
    or merely silent screams

squawkings of a degenerate
dimensions crossed
with leaps and bounds
not caring what is stepped on

soul searches always expose
what you don't want to know
they always give revelations
you can never accept

5

where is the sunset
    how long must it wait
    when you think you're ready
    for the last waning beams
    to filter through
    it just seems to hang on forever

    you are ready
    all the day's work is done
    all the words said and written
    all the preachings have been
    been given to the masses
    all the messages read

    where is the sunset
    how long must it wait

    time is over
    things are done.

6

summer begins with a quiet rush
    gently the breeze starts the movement
    in the leaves and the grasses
    along the stream bed
    the water's flow slows very slightly
    disguising the current
    into invisibility
    the insects darting across
    leaving ringlets in their wake
    quickly the trout moves in for the table
    reserved
    the chain of life circulates
    and the breeze gently starts the movement
    in the leaves and the grasses
    along the stream bed

7

paradise and prejudice

golden dreams washed with
    butterfly kisses and hummingbird wings
    gentle breezes stirring through
    strands free of trusses and bands

    swings in the moonlight
    with laughter and kicking
    rolling in the grass
    or wallowing in the leaves

    paradise and prejudice

    walks in the surf
    waves crashing about
    hand in hand
    strolling in the dark

    falling in the sand
    with kisses exciting
    raising the temperature
    of the blood

paradise and prejudice

the laughter of love
fills all the senses
emotions soar to new heights
with each successive touch

bells ring westminster rhymes
as sound is deafened
by the pounding
of the heart

paradise and prejudice

dances with bodies entwined
fluid motion flowing together
in unison
movement matching movement

physically altering the states
of the individuals
to become a single
blended soul

paradise and prejudice

8

steeped canyon walls
    guarding the treasure
    buried at the spring

    pastel paintings
    diffused with light
    applied with strokes
    delicate yet foreboding

    the artist lived
    each sunset
    reveled each moon rise
    counted the stars exactingly

turned to the canvas
put his poetry in color
his passion
behind the walls and in the crevices

enough just to peek through
to entice the viewer
to dig a little deeper
to search for the treasure

buried at the spring
in the steep walled canyons

9

clouds carry the message
   of Socrates and Plato
   written in the pen and ink
   haiku of the sun

   in wonderment
   i try to decipher
   their meanings
   so long lost in translations

   does the thinker
   think the thought
   or the thought the thinker
   is he just a channel

   old thoughts resurface as new
   although with a certain familiarity
   and each philosopher
   claims them as their own

   clouds carry the message
   of Socrates and Plato
   written in the pen and ink
   haiku of the sun

10

chasing butterflies

catching rainbows

chasing butterflies
    while they gently light
    to dance in the nectar
    running like a child
    here to there
    there to here
    laughing and shouting
    with abandon
    finally falling in the grass
    in exhaustion
    only to have the butterfly
    land in your outstretched hand
    you marvel at the colors
    the slight variations
    the lightness of it's touch

the magic powder
that makes tinker bell fly
lightly dusts your palm
you dream of joining
the butterflies and the birds
you long to fly
you open your hand
you've caught a rainbow

11

essence of strawberries

walking with the illustrators
    deciding where the line begins and ends
    creating a new reality
    where all the rules are new

    shall the sun be blue and the moon green
    shall the flowers grow from the air
    and the rocks as buds on the trees
    the choice is ours- mine and the illustrators

    let's color a page
    with purple carnations
    just to see if the editors notice
    let's skate on snowcones
    and lick the syrup as it melts
    let's hide in the corner
    until the wolves are all gone

the poets verse will start the scenario
we'll capture the spirit
and add our own colorization
to the black and white stills

the sun belongs in the garden
the moon belongs to the sea
or is it the rose belongs in the shadows
and the daffodils belong at the shore

the stars they give you forever
the clouds set fantasy free
or is it clouds block the future
and stars burn to brightly to see

i'll walk with the illustrators
we'll decide where the line ends and begins
we'll paint our own stage drops
and to hell with the editors

12

sensuality

  an iris in full bloom
slow dancing naked
finger traces along the lips

nips at the ear
tongue tracing the neck
soft jazz

obscene phone calls from a lover
blow jobs waiting for a train to pass
the feel of satin in the dark

the feel of satin period
light scratches at the small of the back
touching toes and finger tips

brushing the hair of your lover
warm sun on bare breasts
eyelash kisses on nipples

the glow of the candle reflected in your lovers eyes
teasing to hardness with light blowing kisses

whipped cream and cherries
sweet incense and oils
giggles of anticipation
lying close front to back

a nipple poking through silk
cascading hair in the breeze
kisses in water falls

licking wine from fingertips
raindrops on bare skin
sponge baths with bubbles

writing poetry together   naked
fantasies verbalized
massages of seduction

trading glances across the room
licks behind the knee
words whispered breathlessly

the curve of a breast
moans of desire

kisses under water

making love in the sweet grass

clouds

13

secrets whispered in the morning

promises made in the dark

   tell me your name
       lean close and whisper the passion of last
       night
       the sun beacons the moment
       remember the promises made with eyes closed

       a time when caresses were the measure of
       truth
       when passion meant completion
       and whimpers a symbol of trusting
       giving wholly a split second of promise

look to my eyes
let yours convince me they are real
sincerity not embellished
but worn as an emblem of honesty

tell me your secrets
your cherished wants
treasured under lock and key
warehoused in your vaults and catacombs

you earned mine

14

county dances held in the neighbors barn
> brings visions of young girls with braided hair
> full skirts and tight blouses
> to show off the recently developed breasts

> scrubbed faces of the boys
> with nicks from an unexperienced razor
> at the curve of the jaw where it meets the chin
> smelling to much of old spice and tobacco

> the lines formed to stare across the hollow
> each one wishing another would make the first move
> anticipation building as the music drones
> with the beat slightly out of time

> pulling straw from the hair
> straightening the clothes
> and fixing the lipstick
> and with shy giggles holding hands

> somehow not caring about the beat out of time.

15

miracles

miracles persist in alienating the soul
    droppings of ancient mariners and pilgrims
    clutter the passageways and chambers
    used for storage and safe keeping

    the defecation causing imbalance
    the urine a stench which invades every crevice
    and lingers on the clothes
    of everyone who passes too close

    clouding the path until the goal is out of focus
    the object of the search is forgotten
    replaced by a false sense of security
    and a promise of earthly and heavenly
    pleasures

    the droppings stick to the skin
    working their way into the very pores
    to gain a hold cell by cell
    invading one molecule at a time

quietly the thinker sits pondering
all the questions of the past and future
all the screams and whimpers
the whispers uttered in the midnight
he schemes and dreams with hope
the future seems bleak
and the droppings edge their way
closer to his heart

the cancer that eats his very existence
birthing the desolation where he feels
comfortable
the solace he breathes for
enables him to discredit all views but his own

16

seaside vistas explored on a whim
    the surf sounding as an ancient drum
    keeping the cadence
    moving closer

    eyes fixed on the horizon
    watching for the faintest glimpse
    of things withheld
    things dreamed on fanciful days

    pirate ships were the gulls in mock battles
    dipping and soaring to attack both fore and aft
    the screams as the fallen
    were overwhelmed in defeat

a ships captain stands on the bow
as the freighter churns out of port
off to new adventures in distant lands
where dark complexioned girls sit combing
their hair

the kites soar as the fighter pilots
maneuver the planes in aerial feats
destined to make the ladies faint
and all the young men jealous

17
illusions

sequined gowns form the basics of illusion
strapless bras giving support where needed
and adding definition to contour and dreams
expectations and desires

the dancers whirl to the waltzes and fox-trots
fluidity in a motion keeping time
masking themselves in an air of sophistication
be-jeweled in diamond dripping with fantasy

the young men buttoned in cummerbunds
think only of stripping away
the falsehoods to expose the true beauty
the nakedness and the lust

they play the role of partner
of consort of confidant and brother
all the while wondering what treasures
lay hidden between the legs of their companions

18

owl woman goes walking

owl woman goes walking
    steps as silent as wings in the night
    seem to glide on the grasses
    and petals themselves

    sensations of sexuality
    cause vibrations shaking
    the very essence of believing
    the very knowledge of knowing

    she walks in the shadows
    clinging to the edges to seek balance
    to find the neutrality of harmony
    the qualifications of ecstasy

    gendered as one complete
    to experience the pleasures and passions
    the pains of the whole
    known to none

talons interpret questions
to qualify answers given
in clouds and mists
formed to inhibit circulation

she steps lightly as not to awaken dreams
owl woman goes walking
she visits the haunts and perches
long abandoned in the pursuit of self
the paths overgrown with weeds of confusion

she sees with clarity
yellow eyes piercing the fogs
to catch a movement of a mouse
a beat of a heart

she knows without being taught
she lives without caution
trusting only herself as the whole
spirit infused in the core

sensual as the dancer
she entices the passion from it's hiding place
among the sweetgrass along the waters edge
a handful of water to quench the thirst

she sings the song of experience
known pleasures explored with
the burning of body and soul
merged in the fire of balance

she whispers as not to awaken dreams

owl woman goes walking
the light in visions
grows dark and confused
as she hands the passion to her lover

he knows the taste of her breasts
her scent compounds the complexion
to a rainbow washing across the tips
as her nipples grow in the suckling

her touch charged with current
as she explores his body
with her fingertips
her tongue tracing his muscles

he knows the pleasure
of her penetration
as she changes in the middle
woman to man

she challenges his authority
and he falls in a heap on the grasses
he knows the touch of balance
he feels the woman inside growing

she caresses to console his confusion

owl woman goes walking
she speaks with dreams
visions of gender mixed with metaphors
destined to balance spirit

her lover finds sensations
captured in forgotten photographs
images of couplings confused
by breasts and penises

she shares her knowledge
as he discovers
it is his own design
his own interpretation

owl woman goes walking
she smiles

19

RAINBOW SMOKE

silent strings
> as if strummed
> with the breath of a dragonfly
> serenade the morning with colour
>
> dances on the window sill
> around the dust and through the smoke
> billowing across the shafts of sun
> swirling with the music in their heads
>
> eyelids flutter with sparks of life
> arousing passions and heartbeats
> skin tingling in anticipation
> of carresses soon to follow

she sees with blurred vision
the love she feels
his hands cupping her breast
lightly teasing the nipple

the music plays every morning
the same words
the same melody
the same dream

20

    she sits at the turnstile
        counting as they pass
        she looks at their faces
        to catch a glimpse of recognition

        they walk past to be on their way

        seldom does she meet the eye
        no one notices the pursing lips
        or the light smile at the corners
        she hides behind a mask of apathy

        they walk past to be on their way

        the clothes they wear tell stories
        of bank vaults and boardrooms
        of luncheons and bedrooms
        she laughs at the telling

they walk past to be on their way

she sees them clearly
nothing can be hidden
she watches to see pain and hurt
she offers those a kind word

and they walk past to be on their way
millions pass in the counting
day after day the turnstile turns
she takes their ticket
and punches their pass

and they walk past to be on their way

she imagines as lovers
first one then another
the cut of a suit
the curve of a breast

they walk past to be on their way

she longs to be held
caresses light and caring
pleasures left wanting
except in fantasy

and they walk past to be on their way
starlight as neon
glows in her window
she watches the street
counting as they pass

they walk past to be on their way

21

dream just a little dream

close your eyes
> dream just a small dream
> feel yourself begin to float
> with no ballast
> on a sea of clouds
> magic swirling clouds
> of every color imaginable
>
> the colors blend
> with your skin tone
> causing kaleidoscope patterns
> on your fingertips
> you touch the sky
> and the colors are absorbed
> at that very instant

smiles seem abundant
wide toothy grins
and laughter
singing with the voice
of an angel
soprano on the fringe
of a melody

fly with your arms spread
soar in wide curves and arcs
with the eagles as your companions
play tag with the eaglets
as you both test your skill
as aviators and hunters
as friends and lovers

you tire and begin to drift
just letting the currents
carry you towards the horizon
the sunset beacons
with dancers of color
doing a fox-trot
to the tune of a waltz

funny thing with dreams
nothing is out of place
everything fits as it should
with no judges or expectations
take the time to heal your passion
take the time to heal your soul
take the time to dream

just a little dream.

22

sunsets and magic

the first time we ever saw the sunset
    we believed the painters used the sky
    as a canvas of their own design

    they chose the colors in a random mish-mash
    designed to confuse the watchers
    and to keep them in awe of their talent

    the magic of refraction was unknown
    also the tricks of illusion
    we all saw the meanings though

    the artists have all long since
    been replaced by steel and timber
    by concrete and asphalt

    no illusions coincide with the sunset
    no magic is seen through blindered eyes
    no one sees the meanings

23

she stands there just watching
    the colors of the rainbow in her hair
    just to show a mask of defiance
    to the society she feels abandoned her

    the whispers are not for her to hear
    yet how can she not notice the stares
    or the accusations muttered
    with cutting glances

    quality time for quality time
    but where's the quality

    single episodes of gilligan's island
    show how ridiculous society sees
    did the skipper never fuck mary ann
    how about the professor and ginger

    and poor little gilligan
    was he really that dumb
    or did he really have
    the master plan

quality time for quality time
but where's the quality

subjected to the nightly deluge of ozzie and harriet
not to mention leave it to beaver
can anyone not see where
we got our definition of quality

a friend once said
have you ever noticed
that viking ships are all different
yet the vikings are all the same

he really didn't know what he was saying
but it still had the ring of truth
it rang like a giant bronze bell
again to steal his words

the vikings and the warriors
are now relegated to the playing zones
so that we can all cheer for our favorites
in the coliseum and the lions never go home

quality time for quality time
but where's the quality

our children see so much clearer than we

they see the hypocrisy we have grown

so accustomed to accepting

as the foolishness of generations

they've watched and learned

and decided not to repeat history

not to follow in our boot tracks

not to accept what can not be accepted

so she just stands there watching

with the colors of the rainbow in her hair

looking for quality time

from a society that abandoned her.

24

stepping stones blanket the garden path
   the moss oozing between the cracks
   a most luscious green
   looking like velvet feels

25

    did you ever think
        what would happen
        if we could sail on the wind

        if we could see with the eagles
        all the country-side
        for miles and miles

    did you ever think what would happen

    did you ever feel
    the warmth of the campfire
    on a starlit night

the sparks flying about
to carry the messages
to the heavens

did you ever think what would happen

did you ever dream of mornings
rainbows or kisses

did you ever think what would happen

26

variations of a theme

    the dancers whirl to
        their own deviations
        like the patrons of a whore house

        each wants a fantasy
        to fulfill their own
        expectations

        but expectations go wanting
        in a world of fantasy

27

sage bends as
    a bitter wind rakes the sand
    formations of doom on a landscape
    where desolation is singular

    colors blend as the sunrise awakens
    and the blossoms greet the warmth
    in colors as varied as the artists' palette
    mixed in an abstract mish-mash

    seen through the eyes of a novice
    a beetle scampers on a random course
    first this way then that
    as if in a drunken stupor

    the eyes of the novice are mine
    the shapes bent to seemingly fit
    what ever form i desire
    if only i knew just what my desires were

    paths i chose eventually lead nowhere
    behind the doors are hidden only more doors

the questions answered by questions
are the ends ever a reward for the means

the cost is not too dear so they say
but none have ever given what i have
how can they judge the cost to me
how do they determine just what is too dear

the madman surfaces at the most inopportune times
spouting his metaphors and clichés

and flaunting his most base desires

while preaching spirituality

preaching, preaching, preaching

can the madman exist

without the permission of the masses

without the support of the critics

so many questions, so many questions

go out and play, don't bother us now

such an inquisitive young man

you don't always have to ask why

still the sage bends

in a bitter wind that rakes the sand

28

lavender eyes

she stands at the edge
    with her arms outstreched
    as if to catch the sea spray
    falling about her

    the wind moving her hair
    in billowing torrents
    the fabric of her gown
    plastered agianst her skin with wet

    her dreams give the impressions of
    long abandoned kisses
    and caresses with held for ages
    yet hope lingers in her lavender eyes

    she sang the songs of youth
    all the gay songs
    and she danced to the music
    that made her flesh quiver

she would move with the fluid of sensuality
while oblivious to the reaction
she caused in the groins and minds
of the ones who noticed.

they never told her
they only hungered for the
touch of a passion
they could only imagine

so she sat in the parlor
waiting for some justification
of the feelings in her breasts
and the sparkle in her lavender eyes

she would touch her self and dream of
copulations
dogs and horses men and women
the spasms would reach her
only to subside in panting and unrealized
wantings

if only they would touch her
if only they could kiss her
and love her
with tongue in cheek metaphors

growing into a blossom
from a crown of thorns
the lavender of a thistle
attracts the most suspecting suitors

caution given over to self doubts
have driven away the lovers
she wished she could have
she wished she could have

the wave crashes agianst her
the thin cloth outlines her breasts
as she holds the lover to her
the cold sea to touch and excite her

dreams and dancers
with lavender eyes.

29

glowing embers
    light your face
    with radiance
    and warmth

    sitting on this rock
    across the fire
    no words
    thoughts turned inward

    just watching

    a slight curve of the lip
    remembering the events
    of the day

    a small stick
    poking in the coals
    stirring more
    than the fire

your skin getting rosy
from the heat
seems to become
even more alive

with eyes sparkling

as a flame

slowly licks

at a log

roasted marshmallows

a piece of chocolate

gently squeezed between

graham crackers

the favorite food

relegated to camps

along the shore

time passes so slowly

waiting for the fire

to die

just watching.

30

 powder soft
  falling in
  torrents unheard
  covering the landscape

  streetlights cast
  eerie halos in the night
  illuminating the
  silent deluge

  all sounds are muffled
  no voice carries
  even the cars passing
  go silent along their way

bundled and warm
walking down
past the steepled church
glowing through the stained glass

angels in the courtyard
with no explanation
of origin
wings and gowns in the snow

31

questions go unanswered
    the truth confused by the subject matter
    seems to shrink before the connotations
    uttered by jealous peeping toms

32

i stand naked in the moonlight
    the water lapping at my ankles

    a hint of peppermint
    rekindles memories
    scenes brought to life
    with backseat kisses
    and foggy windows
    and the bra straps
    that never come undone

    i've thought of her often
    the girl not quite a woman
    yet excited by the touches
    of a new born sexuality
    inhibited only by innocence
    long passionate kisses
    and lingering touches

    somewhere the innocence
    turned to knowing

33

willows

a slight bend in the river
    allows the sand to wash
    across the roots

    the trailings reaching down
    to plant themselves in soil
    less than fertile

    another life born
    of sun, sand and water.

34

visions
    of
sugar plums
dancing
in dreams

happiness
and
laughter
bursting
at seams

childhood
fancies
sweetened
yet
shelved

christmas
mornings
eyes
full of
delight

halloweens'
goons
and
goblins
all the
wonderful
frights

childhood
fancies
sweetened
yet
shelved

sun filled
days
lazy
and long

secret forts
tree houses
godzilla
king kong

childhood
fancies
remembered

35

prisms glistening
    diffusing the light
    into a myriad of colors
    rainbows dancing
    on the wall.

    sunbeams enveloped
    and dissected to minute scale
    pleasing to the eye

    warmth surrounding
    fluttering eyelids
    lying in the sun
    with a daydream
    playing through

soft flowing strings
quiet rhythms
gliding smoothly
to relax built tensions

afternoons spent napping
holding close the security
and the passion
of time spent together

happiness simply passing the time

36

Do you remember?

> Long ago in
> a far away land
> it seems
>
> The dreams are still there
> still smoldering
> inside
> not yet lost forever
>
> Do you remember?
>
> The dreams of passion
> The dreams of peace

The hopes and fears
of cliches
uttered as a child

Do you remember?

Pastel sunsets
at the shore
the call of
a loon at a misty twilight

Do you remember?

They are all still there
and each cherished
because shared
with you.

37

When we're sixty - four, a very interesting thought.
Will you still need me, will you still feed me?
The feed I'm not too concerned about. The
need is a different story.

                Songs of love
                the birds sing
                Songs of love
                the wind whispers
                Songs of love
                my very being
                depends on you.

Feelings. A very over used lounge song.
                The meaning
                says so much
                more than the words
                ever express
                The pure spiritual
                feeling of
                true love.

The endless row to hoe.
                    Everyday chores
                    seem not
                    so mundane
                    Everyday events
                    take on special
                    meaning
                    Just by being with you.

When we're sixty - four.
I hope you'll still need me.
I hope you'll still feed me.
I hope the love never ends

38

dreams
> wandering through
> a darkened hall
> or skipping through
> brightly lit fields.
>
> they always reveal
> what's in the soul.
>
> words
> spoken soft
> and low
> or harshly
> spit out in
> fits of rage.

they always reveal
what's in the soul.

dreams or words
which are real
does it really matter?

words or dreams
spoken and they're
the same.

truth

the words are there
as are the dreams
but which are which

dreams.

39

Brute force
>   hell bent and bound
>   the conquest made
>   forcibly
>
>   Brute force
>   grabbing and clutching
>   coverings torn
>
>   Brute force
>   entrances
>   made with disregard
>
>   Brute force
>   release but
>   no satisfaction
>
>   Brute force
>   tears flowing
>   uncontrollable sobs
>
>   shattered lives left in the street.

40

dark stormy clouds threaten
    the small perfect valley
    dank walls of the cliffs
    with highlighted shimmerings

    greys in the sky
    contrast starkly
    with the yellows and reds
    of the new wild flowers

    trees growing exactingly
    not a branch out of place
    the blending of the shades perfect
    add a frame to the valley

a small stream moving
on to meet it's siblings
growing larger as it comes nearer
trout feeding in a small pool

the vision beheld
almost surrealistic
moving folding into itself
seen in the late afternoon

paints lend the texture
slowly the canvas comes alive.

41

laying here
    poetry writing itself
    not knowing how the
    words come

    complex manipulation of verses
    spew forth without thought
    forming themselves
    as the pen glides across the pad

    sweet sensuous phrases
    excite the paper
    heating the fibres
    to the core

the form saying
as much as the connotation
hidden meanings
double entendres

laying here
the poetry writing itself
not even knowing
why the words come.

42

sarcastic remarks
    said not in jest
    flash points reached
    with just a glance
    unrest surrounds
    the unwary

    violence with the smoke
    beatings in the street
    grandmothers bleeding at the curb
    weeping for their babies
    the intolerance of the children

    soldiers guarding the grain
    the warlords profit
    while babies slowly starve
    begging for a cup of meal
    mothers breast no longer giving

    here we sit
    watching the horror
    tubes turned to daily stories
    it's the others
    it's not me

young with shaved heads
crucify any that are different
bring back memories
of times all but forgotten
scenes of hatred

religions are the one right thing
each to themselves
fighting for god
has always been the best cause
each believing they were correct

and here we sit
watching the horror
tubes turned to the daily stories
it's the others
it's not me

has apathy grown
or has it just become more visible
troubles in a far away land
seen on the nightly news
so far away so it never happen to me

warnings ignored

children dead in the school yard
color of the clothes
the only difference
the bullets not really caring

and here we sit
watching the horror
tubes turned to the daily stories
it's the others
it's not me

the channel gets changed
some mindless chatter
escapism for millions
at least for thirty minutes
our thoughts are occupied

the children are asking
where ours morals have gone
our ethics have vanished
with my mother the car
packed in the vault of a millionaire

if the warnings ignored
here we'll sit watching the horror
we'll be the others — our children the dead.

43

canoe

    learning from a master
    the turn of a paddle
    in silence

    using the current
    to guide the bow
    nuances of kneeling
    for the most powerful stroke

    quietly gliding
    through the reeds
    to see sights
    astonishing

    runs over
    beaver dams
    with speed
    without grace

    shooting the rapids
    adrenalin running wild
    placement of the blade

summers spent in solitude
listening to the loons
the mink and the king fisher
chilly nights
gazing at stars
northern lights
astounding

ghost stories
strange tracks on the shore
debating forever
the meaning of religion

meditations enlightened
auras explored
meeting the guides
the shaman the teacher

friendships refound
incarnations discovered
relating to all

44

sequined dreams dance in the moonlight
    sparkles delighting mindless heros
    each reaching for the brass ring held
    within the tight grasps of illusion

    silent emotions emanate in miraculous colors
    exploding in auras surrounding the bodies
    as the souls escape their earthly hold
    sullen depression turns to an ashen hue

    the release completed easily
    when the time is appropriate
    at the very instant predestined
    the life is completed as written

    as the mourning runs it's course
    the actions and the possessions
    are evaluated as the greatness of the soul
    by those left to wonder

each sees the accumulation
the ultimate indicator of success
each uses the indication as an excuse
to qualify their own existence

mistaken assumptions cloud even
the most illuminated mind
worldly acquisitions glitter in the light
and mesmerize all who pass by

the quality of existence is measured
not by the material possessions acquired
and not by the deeds deemed great by others
when all is said and done

existence is measured by love.

45

blessings

secret gardens full
    with rosebuds and butterflies
    honeysuckle on the vine
    fragrances mixing to new perfumes

    spring rains suddenly appearing
    drenching to the skin
    tears of laughter uncontrollable
    while scurrying for cover

    playing before the fire
    with tickles and hugs
    wrestling on the rug subtly
    ignoring the overtones

    lazy afternoons spent
    holding and just talking
    dreaming and scheming
    for some south sea paradise

quiet evenings reading not having to speak
an occasional touch cementing the bond
already unbreakable by the years
and the many lives played before

hurrying to meet for a quick bite
dedicating moments previously reserved
changing agendas with a last minute call
smiling when the eyes first meet

sneaking away for private weekends
exploring trails and roads not much more
losing the way by taking a short cut
and ending up making love under a tree

seductions in the backseat
did we really go to see the movie
making children with the moment
lost in passion

quiet walks at the new year
looking at houses in the windows
listening to firecrackers pop
welcoming in the new calender

the blessings are counted easily
only one finger is necessary
to measure all the wonders of the universe
my blessings are all you.

46

iron pickets
> protect the garden
> all the flowers
> dead from the cold
>
> the beauty is still there
> lying dormant until
> the first spring rain
> revives the sleeping sprouts
>
> winter shaves close
> to the roots
> sometimes too close
> and revival is impossible

47

flickering light from a candlestick
    bearskin rug before a fire
    wine goblets on the end table
    romance like an aura about the room

    warmth

48

soft lace
    on the collar framing
    the sweet line of the neck
    lightly covered by tumbling curls

    wide eyed astonishment
    feeling the tug
    of the first fish
    pulled from the lake

    watching a butterfly
    float from bud to bud
    sipping the nectar
    with fluttering wings

    blowing dandelion crowns
    searching for four leaf clovers
    pulling petals
    he loves me he loves me not

hours on the telephone
talking of boys
and "how could she
ever like him"

first loves
so devastated
death is certain
until a new boy smiles

so grown up
dressing for the prom
corsages and boutonnieres
gowns made not for little girls

the things a father sees.

49

innocents and visionaries

growth cumulated with understanding
    appeasements given freely with passion
    unleashed the locks fall open
    the walls begin to crumble

    burning touches as caressed by the sun
    excite and demand response
    opening the pores
    allowing the energy to flourish

    small titillations
    mindless and unknowing
    become focused
    as the cause of the flow

    has the visionary become the innocent

questions without answers
asked to provoke thought
to create light for the
darkest corner

the path brilliantly lit
in colors and hues
too vibrant for description
bathe eyeless gazes

percussions and brass synthesized
auditory delights stimulate movements
of body and soul opening passages
long clogged and closed

has the innocent become the visionary

the demon the goddess
the student the mentor
the lover the healer
the questions the answers

innocents and visionaries

+1

I'm an old man.

Have been all my life. An old, white man accused of social privilege and widely accepted as a vile perpetrator of bigotry.
I don't remember it, but it must be there.
I can see where some of the claims are justified. I can see where the accusations may be warranted.

I remember the line stretched in the stream, jerking with the tug of mutilation. Pulling the barb, worrying more about the cost of the hook than the pain of the trout.
I remember the guns, the blood of the bird leaking into the ground. The deer crumpled, neck twisted where it fell. Lifeless eyes staring back at me, slightly glazed.
The voices for nature cry for retribution.
I'm vilified
But, weren't they there for us? Weren't they food?
Not now, of course. But times have changed.

Every time I hear a person of color speak of their trials; their complaints against the society I created, I cringe at the assault. And it is an assault. Rightly so, I suppose, but I don't remember being the justification. I don't remember casting the downtrodden under the grinding wheels. I don't remember placing myself on a pedestal of social climbing assholes.

But I suppose I did.

A black child, thumbing through books that contain no image of themselves. Do they even wonder what the dominant color is? Is there a question, or is it permanently displayed on the printed page as Dick and Jane and Baby? Blond-haired, blue-eyed Baby.

I don't remember pulling a flesh colored crayon and seeing the representation of my skin. I just never thought about it. Flesh was a color. I didn't notice that flesh was the color of my friends, my family. I didn't notice it wasn't the color of Issac, the color of his family.

I suppose I should have. I thought of Isaac as Isaac. I didn't notice what his color was, he was Isaac. I never noticed, he and his two sisters, were the only black kids at school. I never thought about it. I didn't notice Isaac's flesh wasn't flesh.

But I suppose I should have. I wonder if he did?

I can see the point. I didn't notice it before, but it's there.

I had a lover, once.

She reminds me of warm summer nights and skinny-dipping at the pond. I haven't seen her for years, but she's there. The curves of her body glistening in the moonlight. Her breasts rising as she bobbed, treading water just beyond my reach. Her laughing eyes, as she splashed the sun-warmed water.

I see her every day. I can't remember her name, but I can remember her nipples, puckered just above the waterline.

She taught me things. Two years older, she had seen so much more than I ever would.

As I think of her now, she was just doing what was expected. What a girl did to have a friend, a boy of her own.

Times were different then. When she asked if I loved her, of course, I said yes. Her body was on display, her touch ignited my passion.

Of course, I loved her.

But I can't remember her name. What does that make me? I may have pushed, but isn't that what happens when you get naked at fourteen?

I didn't force her, I didn't rape her.

Did I?

I fucked her. She fucked me.

Wasn't it what was expected?

That's what we did, country kids, skinny-dipping in the pond.

Maybe I should have noticed the tears a little sooner.

Maybe I should have remembered her name.

Now I see women rallying, pushing against the expected fondling and I can't believe anyone would allow such disrespect. How could a man make advances, move heaven and earth, just to peek at a nipple, caress a thigh? Just to satisfy an urge, a thought, a fantasy.

I see women flinch when I look at them, pull their blouse closed and turn away.

I don't remember staring, but I feel my cheeks flush. I don't remember an unwanted touch.

But I don't remember her name, either.

I'm an old man … just an old man.

My flesh is flesh colored. My sex dominates, I have a penis. That's acceptable, isn't it?

I didn't cause this…this state of society. It wasn't my choice. I did what was expected, what was normal.

Someone else…

I'm not the cause, am I? I don't remember bigotry. I don't remember rape.

But, I'm an old man. There's a lot I don't remember.

I did what was expected. Cutting of trees, tilling the soil, moving water to meet my needs.

It's history. And history is always written by the winner.

It's my story. It's what I remember.

I'm an old white man that didn't know better. Same as my grandfather and his grandfather and his grandfather and his.

I've nurtured my son to replicate what should be, what has been, like my father did—

but he's different...

He doesn't see the need. Maybe it's not there anymore.

Times have changed.

And I'm just an old man

Dedication

and

Acknowledgements

There's something to be said for time. Things become more clear, not necessarily crystal clear, but not quite as clouded and fuzzy.

Words are the magic that bind creative process; imagery and form.

These poems are dedicated to time without which they would still be an unopened manuscript.

Without the words the imagery would be meaningless.

dhd